Thoughts I Never Shared

Rachel Ragan

BookLeaf Publishing

Presentation by *BookLeaf Publishing*

Web: www.bookleafpub.com

E-mail: info@bookleafpub.com

ISBN: 9789357210287

First edition 2022

Hope

Hope is a living thing
That brings light
Even in the darkest night

A burning ember hiding away
Until it needs to burn bright as day
It never dies, only bides

When all seems lost and good things no more
The ocean is drowning all of you
Hope springs up, a light shining the way to shore
To save a soul, a life, to renew

Hope is a living thing
And breath is all it needs
As long as there is life to sing
There is hope, a living seed

Pain

Pain is an unwanted companion
Sometimes a jailer
Sometimes a vast canyon
Separating from those who don't understand
Never to leave
Never to breathe
Merely to trap
Those who cannot conceive
A life free from its clutch
A life without the touch
Of its miserly hand
A strong, tight band
That never releases
Those it decreases
To nothing but pieces in pain

Alone

The silence overwhelmingly loud
The pounding of your heart
The wind of the breath in your lungs
Sheer peace, melancholy, and agony
Sorrow for what is gone
Joy for what is present
The one state of being we love and hate
Alone

Almost

Chemistry unrealized
Potential left hanging
What friendship unknown

Lovers or soulmates
Romantic, kindred spirits
Connections unknown

Sisters or brothers?
No blood connection needed
What family they lost

For want of a word
A moment of time, a thought
Potential is gone

What was wanted is
No longer available
Gone forevermore

Lost to the abyss
The vast space of the unknown
possibilities

Almost romantics

Almost friends, family, coworkers
Almost, never here

Who I Was

I miss who I was
Before my world was shattered
Before my body gave out
Back then, such different things mattered

I didn't worry about getting up
I didn't worry about being able to drive
I wanted to dance and play and sing and fill my cup
I felt and saw and lived and I was alive

Now I am a shell
I cannot do things like before
I count the times I fell
I don't know if I will ever be more

My body gave out
My soul is barely there
My heart feels like it's in drought
I don't know that I care

My days run together
My life is a blur
Is this for forever?
The thought makes me gasp for air

I miss the laughter and fun
I miss the movement and action
I miss the friends and the sun
I miss the me before my adaption

Who was I before?
I was ambitious and driven
I was joyful and never a bore
I had places to go and I had a vision

Now I just dream
Of who I was
Of the theme
Of the me that was

Drowning

Take a breath and feel your lungs fill.
The liquid burns where there should be air.
The world is blue and still
Strangely peaceful, not fighting, no more to
bear.

The light beckons above, shimmering in a haze
as the dark below offers sweet release.
Can you feel yourself drowning far from the
sun's gaze?
Do you succumb to the sweetness and peace?

Do you turn towards the shimmering light?
It draws you in until your head breaks the
surface and you feel the air on your skin.
The gushing of water from your lungs as you try
not to give in.
The sweet breath of air reminds of all that is
bright.

Drowning again just to live.
All is washed away and a new birth for you
as you awaken with a purpose anew.
You have to live, you have more to give

Gasping, you swim for the shore
You leave behind the worries and the pain.
All you have is to gain.
The world is yours once more!

Plans to Keep

I saw my future full of joys
Possibilities endless, limitless
Anything was mine, like a box of toys
I tried everything and nothing, frivolous

My only goal was experiences
My only thought to explore it all for me
I never sought to understand vicarious
Joy and excitement all to see

My future today is far more bleak
My whole future shattered in one fell swoop
My choices all seem weak
No longer anticipation, just hoop after hoop

Then one morn the sun broke bright
And changed my whole view
No longer dark and clouded by night
My future suddenly seemed new

No athletic feats, no more dance or cleats
But arts and smarts and psychology
I can still work and play, just no waltzing
through the streets

I can still do the things I want, just from a new topography

I mourned the death of the dreams I left
In the wake of my healthy self
In morning light I was no more bereft
I dusted off the dreams I had on the shelf

The dreams became a new goal
I had no more time to weep
My days began with a new soul
I had plans to keep

I have plans to keep
I have joy found true
Although the road is steep
I will these hopes and plans pursue

Joy Through Despair

Joy through despair
finds its way in the darkest lair
It lightens the heaviest air

The darkness cannot overcome
The spark of joy that softly thrums
and lets all who hear it know
that joy itself will surely show

When the world crashed down
all you knew is shattered on the ground
the light comes pouring in to show the pattern in the round

Mosaics made from shattered pieces of the past
Futures built on shattered glass
Joy drives all to show
You are worth more than you know

Joy comes in the darkest night
When despair steals the light
The air is gone and you can't breathe
Joy brings light and love and ease

Joy through despair fights its way

to show you how to live another day
Joy will keep you anchored through the dark
Keep you alive and leave its mark

Someday

Someday calls me softly
Bids me listen and follow
The thrill pulls me awfully
The excitement impossible to swallow

The life I want, the life I am creating
Time spent discovering, investigating
The work is now so the joy can come
Of a labor done in love, well done

The sounds of someday linger in my ear
What I want, what I can do, the time draws near
For the plans to come to fruition
It's the start of a brand new mission

Someday calling, someday beckons
Someday comes with force to reckon
I stand prepared and steady
Bring on someday, I am ready!

Yesterday Coming

Yesterday coming
Nowhere to hide, no stopping it
Your past will come back

Tomorrow is paused
Caught in the tides of memories
Joy or pain, it's there

Yesterday coming
No warning, no request, just there
Caught you by surprise

Thought you were okay
Memories strike on a good day
Steal your breath away

A moment in time
Haunts your mind, caught up in a bind
Where you stay inside

Yesterday coming
Without warning or grace, no space
Yesterday just came

The Night Road

Driving the night road
Blinding headlights shining bright
Nothing much in sight

Stars above shining
Incandescent, light the night
Just being there so bright

Turn off the engine
Contemplate, thought provoking sight
Vast night sky, small me

Who am I? Here, now?
Who was I, who will I be?
Who will care but me?

Sitting by the road
Taking off a load, pondering
Life, by the night road

The Call of the Void

The call of the void seems so sweet
All the places and people you could meet
The pain will be gone, then you'll be free
If only it were just temporary

The call of the void is so strong
You've been holding on so long
You know you can't let go
You will never let it show

The strain is great and you're tired and sore
You want a break, want to walk through the door
The timings' not right, the actions' a sin
You'll never let go, you'll never give in

No matter how strong the call will become
You'll be stronger still, it cannot be done
You have a reason, you have a conviction
This temporary solution is simply a fiction

There is no resolution or end
There is no peace for the one who steps in
The sun is coming back out again
Just hold on and let it warm up your skin

The call of the void is strong, this is true
But it never will ever be stronger than you
It is momentary in its pull, you can wait for the next lull
You can hold on to the light, and hope for a glimpse of sun through the night

The call of the void will hold no power over you
You have a stronger power to hold to
Jesus is greater and shows his love
You hold to the strength loaned from above

The call of the void lessens each day
The sun shines brighter as you step away
You will step forward in hope
That you never reach the end of your rope

You have a purpose and places to go
For the call of the void, you'll be a no-show
You step forth into light
You keep going, shining so bright

Communication

Communication changed for me
I could not say what I would think
A haze in my brain, a fog too dense to see

The words were there, then swallowed
The sentence clear, then not
I felt like I just wallowed

A vast abyss of letters
Nothing made a word
Nothing made it better

When it became clear
When I could speak
No one seemed to hear

Cutting off sentences
Rushed to finish
No care for my preferences

Put in a box, locked, throw away the key
No chance to redeem or heal
This is now and forever me

No one lets you grow

No one lets you show
That what once was, is no more

Just because you failed before
Doesn't mean you fail evermore
You heal and change and grow

Given the chance, you could show
How far you have come
From what you were and what you've done

No one cares, no one listens
Locked in your box
Teardrops glisten

Your world shrank as they fell away
No one takes the time of day
If they don't talk, why should you?

The effort shouldn't be just from you
Communication is a two way street
You'd think you could meet

But life doesn't work that way
So you move off toward a sunny day
You laugh and talk and play

Without their judgement or their glares
Without their laughter or their stares

The butt of the joke you'll be no more

They can walk right out the door
You've got better things to do
Keep on moving, walk on through

They'll all see some bright day
Just because you struggled to talk
Your brains didn't take a walk

You can still think and feel
You're not a child to be brought to heel
You have life to live and much to offer

You can fill your own coffer
Nothing to beg, nothing to ask
You will fill your own glass

You will complete your task
Get up when you're knocked on your ass
You will live a life that's full

Grab the horns of the bull
Feel joy and pride and confidence
Plan and build your own fence

Boundaries for your own health
You don't have to share the wealth
Just live life to your best

Don't worry what they say,
They don't matter anyway
You did it all, You can attest

You lived life your very best
When you lay your head to rest
You can say you did your best

Music

Music brought smiles
Over miles and miles
Of effort and toil
Through years of soil
Upon my soul and my body too
What would I do without you?

Music came and lifted me up
Music filled my empty cup
Energized and helped me cope
Gave me joy and brought me hope
I share the joy it brought me
Maybe someone else will see
Some of the pleasure
That I treasure
All found in music

Feelings

How you feel is justified
You don't have to change your mind
You can be frustrated
You can feel elated
You don't have to hide or dilute
You are you; what they think is moot
You have the right to your life
You have the right to respond to strife
You can't act illegally
But you can feel how you please
It's your feeling, they can't say
How you choose to feel or say
What you should process today
You are you and that's enough
You don't have to explain your gruff
They can deal
You can heal
It's your life
Not their strife
How you feel is justified
Only you has to be satisfied

Life in a Blink

Life moves at a fast pace
If you blink you'll miss a moment
Sometimes it feels like a race
Sometimes we're suspended in space
Nowhere to go, nothing to show
Just hovering on the brink
Too much time to think
Relive the past, plan the future
Never in the present
Rushing by without a chance
To stop and process the event
Take the time to stop and slow
Look around and get to know
All you see, to watch them grow
Slow down and breathe
Take a moment to ease
Yourself into a space
Where you can relax and be yourself
Life goes by in a blink
Don't lose yourself trying to think
Don't forget to just be
You're the only one to see
The full extent of your life
So enjoy each precious breath
Live your fullest, 'til your death

Friends

Friends are people you can call
in Spring, Summer, Winter, or Fall
Through the seasons of your life,
Friends will come through laughter or strife
Sometimes for life, sometimes for a season
Friends are friends for a reason
To lean on each other
To adventure or relax
You all have each others backs
Joy to share as life moves on
Children, jobs, or marriages
Sometimes rides in carriages
Life's unique and life's a chore
With friends it's never a bore
Friends bring joy instead of strife
If you let them in your life
Those who stay are welcomed in
Closer than family, they are again
Friends who you love as your own
Friends who leave, leave their mark
They stay in your heart
Thankful for the ones you know
Doesn't matter where you grow
You'll make friends through your life
To help you through in joy and strife

Water

If I could sit and watch the water
Ocean, creek, river, or pool
I feel like I found a jewel
Animals like fish or otter
Sometimes stay and swim or float
Sometimes watch the water with its quiet note
Nature has a precious gift
Water never set me adrift
Deep greens and blues, grays and browns
Waterfalls or lakes around
Different water, different sounds
I could sit and watch for days on end
Happy to just listen in
To hear the tinkle of a brook
Or the rushing through a nook
Water, water everywhere
Peaceful feelings brought to bear
Calming, soothing, let me be
Where I can hear the rolling sea
Rain falls down upon the ground
I will gladly lay me down
A background for the perfect nap
A peaceful painting in my lap
Water is my favorite thing
It makes nature seem to sing

It doesn't matter what form it takes
Water makes my soul ache
For a share of the tranquility
Oh for more agility
To walk and hike and explore
To find the waterfalls and more
I would gladly search all day
To seek the water in any way

Flowers

Flowers grow and flowers show
That you can be pretty and still
Offer value to those would know
That joy in the beauty is more than a frill

Lilacs and roses, pinks and blues
Daisies, sunflowers and bluebonnets
So many shades and so many hues
Flowers are natures colorful sonnets

A scented blanket of colors bright
Flowers offer some of nature's perfume
A gift of rainbow colors for your sight
Flowers make you pause when they come in
bloom

Flowers have a language all their own
You can tell the world how you feel
You can show your love with seeds you've sown
Flowers can tell your appeal

There's nothing so varied and so bright
Flowers are everywhere, wild and light
We can learn to be the same
Bright and colorful, untamed

Into the Mist

Into the mist I went
I walked alone, I wasn't sent
As I searched for something new
I called and called and looked for you
I did not know who you were
I just knew that someone would prefer
If this faceless person lost, was found
And returned home, safe and sound
As I went into the mist, there was more that I saw
I soon realized
Everything seemed disguised
This mist of mine was thick and deep
So hard to see, it seemed to seep
Everywhere without a care
I saw things from times gone by
I stopped and stared and wondered why
Then things from present showed up too
I wondered then, who were you?
As I wandered in the mist
I saw the things that I had missed
This mist was not in the woods
There were no lost people or lost goods
This mist was thick in my mind
This brain fog was just a sign

The lost person that I sought
Would never truly be caught
The lost person there was me
Bound in the web of my brain tree
I went into the mist unaware
I soon found that I was there
I was lost in my own thoughts
The mist was my own lock
The help I wanted to give
To help someone else to live
I was trying to give myself
While I was sitting by the shelf
When I finally left the mist
I was back on my own list
I never know when I'll go back
It calls me there without a pack
I stay for hours or for days
You can tell by my gaze
My eyes get glassy and I freeze
There is no response unless I sneeze
I walk alone into the mist
Not knowing I am on the list
Of people there, lost or found
There is no other soul around

Forged in the Fire

There is a strength of mind
Forged in the fire of experience
There is a strength with barely a sign
Can be found with slight variance
With the strong you will align
Life will take its toll
On each and every soul
If you can stand the heat
You'll know you cannot be beat
You'll be forged in the flames
You will hit what you aim
You will stand strong and true
You will find what you pursue
Forged in the fire of life exquisite
There is no prerequisite
Life will lift you up again
Or wash you down the drain
If you can stand the heat
You will know you can't be beat.
Forged in the fire and the flames
Life will never be a game

www.ingramcontent.com/pod-product-compliance
Lightning Source LLC
Chambersburg PA
CBHW051753130826
49812CB00033B/1129